THE HOME EDIT
FOR TEENS

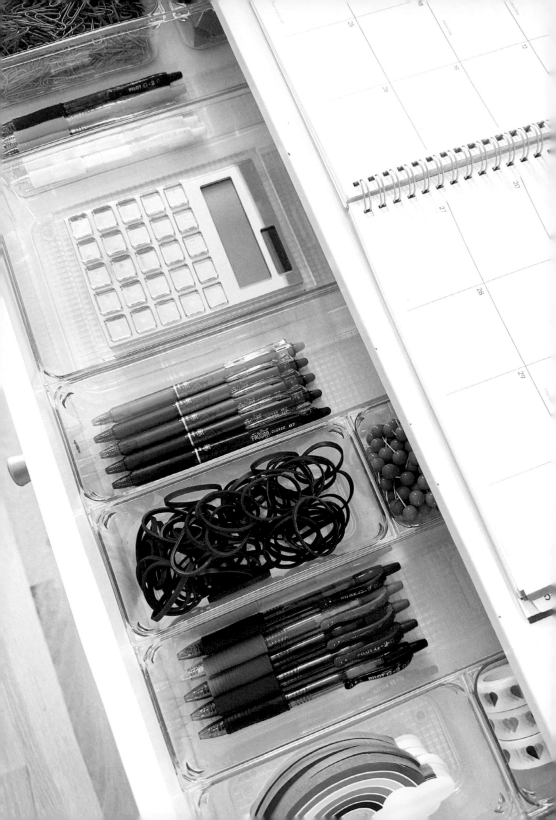

THE HOME EDIT

FOR
teens

how to edit your *space*,
express your *style*, and get things *done*!

CLEA SHEARER & JOANNA TEPLIN

CLARKSON POTTER / PUBLISHERS
NEW YORK

CONTENTS

ALLOW US TO INTRODUCE OURSELVES ♡

We are Clea and Joanna, professional organizers and "cool moms"! Welcome to *The Home Edit for Teens,* where we help you edit your spaces, showcase your unique style, and have a little (okay fine, a lot of) fun along the way!

Seriously, getting organized is *the best,* whether you're curating your closet (page 74) or hosting a sleepover (page 130). First, a space looks *amazing* when organized in rainbow order (page 116). Second, running late for school with *zero idea* where to find your fave sweatshirt is the absolute worst. And finally, organized spaces don't only look better, they actually make us *feel better* (#science)!

JOANNA'S DAUGHTER, MARLOWE!

CLEA'S DAUGHTER, STELLA!

If you are reading this, you most likely fit into one or more of these categories:

1 You Love Organizing

Same! Your bookshelves and sneakers are organized in rainbow order, and whether it's colored pens or lip glosses, you have a pouch for that. Welcome! We promise to take your organizing prowess to new heights with solutions for teen-specific conundrums (like corralling unruly hair accessories) as well as ideas for exciting adventures and parties (camp org! sleepover checklists!). We're so *excited* to make a book just for you. No parents allowed.

2 You Love the *Idea* of Organizing— but Are Not Organized

You mean *not yet*! Being organized comes naturally to some, and for others, it just takes a few super-simple tips to get going. Does your closet feel like an avalanche waiting to happen? We have a system for that! Haven't seen your bathroom countertops (or fave headband) in months? Easy-peasy. Once you start, it's so fun! Next thing you know, you are *looking* for things to organize. Get ready for rooms with rizz. (Did we use "rizz" right?)

3 You Are a Budding Entrepreneur

Calling all mini moguls! As best friends who *love* organizing, we turned our passion into our dream job. And guess what? So can you! It can be an organizing club using all our tips and tricks or a successful lemonade stand (like on page 59).

4 You Are *Our* Kids!

Heyyy, Miles and Marlowe. 🔥🔥 Hiii, Stella and Sutton. 🔥🔥 This book was inspired by you. This book is dedicated to you. We're sorry about the rizz comment. But we love y'all more than organizing in rainbow order. This book is for you.

Let's get started!

Where You *LEARN*

Can school *actually* be cool? Yes, yes it can.
We have tweens (like we said earlier, we're not regular moms, we're cool moms), so we totally get the need for self-expression at school, where, last time we checked, there are one zillion rules to follow. (*Dress codes, amirite?*) That's why we curated tons of creative and colorful spaces, from decked-out lockers to desks that impress, so you can spotlight your unique POV *and* ace the school year.

A ROLLING CART THAT DOUBLES AS A HOMEWORK STATION? TALK ABOUT BUSSIN' (DID WE USE THAT RIGHT?). TURN THE PAGE TO SEE THE TOP TIER!

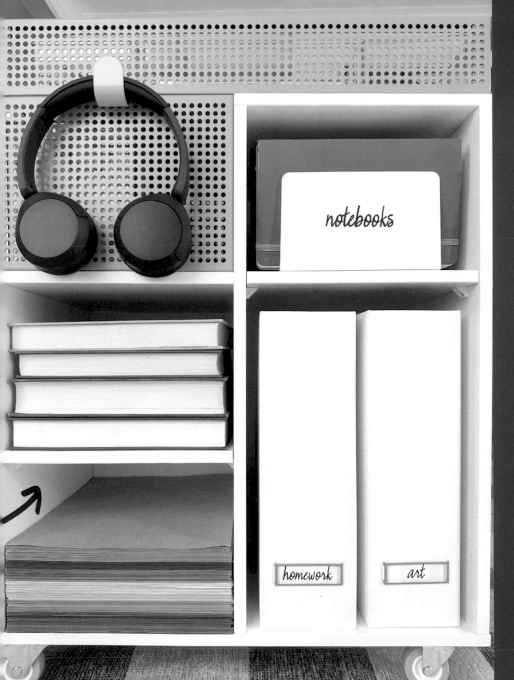

notebooks

homework   *art*

WRITE THIS WAY!

Create divided sections in the top tier of your homework cart or in a desk drawer for pens (in every color, #duh), a calculator, and other supplies you want in easy reach when tackling your worksheets.

A Stress-Free School Year!

Before the first bell rings, get organized so you can do great *and* feel great. The secret sauce: a solid routine! Whether it's homework or skin care, carving out time to get things done ultimately leads to more time for fun (and an extra fifteen minutes of sleep!).

PAPER PLANNERS ROCK FOR MAPPING OUT YOUR WEEK (SEE OUR TEMPLATE ON PAGE 36!).

DON'T FORGET

APPOINTMENT

APPOINTMENT

extra credit

IF YOU'VE
MADE IT TO
THIS SECTION,
YOU DESERVE
A ⭐

GS I DID BUT DIDN'T HAVE TO
(*extra credit*)

THINGS I ABSOLUTELY HAD TO DO ~
SO NEED TO DO NEXT MONTH
(*it's not going to be fine*)

THINGS I DIDN'T DO
(*it's fine*)

LET'S ORGANIZE . . .

night-before-school routine

☐ **GO THROUGH YOUR *ENTIRE* BACKPACK**

Any projects to finish or papers to be signed? Get everything squared away, zipped up, and ready to go in the a.m.

☐ **TAKE INVENTORY OF WHAT YOU HAVE AND WHAT YOU NEED**

This way, you won't have a manic Monday morning! No one wants to remember during homeroom that they are most definitely out of their signature pens.

☐ **DO A QUICK BEDROOM EDIT AND TIDY UP YOUR SPACE**

Does it have to be perfect? Nope. Will it make your morning feel less chaotic? Yep! Plus, Princeton researchers discovered that clutter leads to decreased focus and negative emotions, while an organized space tends to produce positive emotions like calmness and a sense of well-being. Hey, we'll take those vibes!

☐ **SET OUT YOUR CLOTHES (INCLUDING FOR AFTER-SCHOOL ACTIVITIES!)**

So your morning is easy-breezy and your outfit is *on point*. (No one has time to accessorize when they're running late!)

☐ **UNWIND WITH YOUR NIGHTTIME ROUTINE**

From washing your face and brushing your teeth to performing any beauty regimen you have, play your favorite music to elevate the experience!

☐ **CHARGE ANY SCHOOL-RELATED TABLETS**

Make sure any school-related tablets are fully loaded for the next day so you won't be down to the (charging) wire! Speaking of devices: Get them out of your bedroom before you go to bed, and read for thirty minutes before hitting the hay. Your brain will thank you!

☆ Date Completed: _____   ↶ GREAT JOB! FILL IN THE STAR TO TRACK YOUR PROGRESS

Love
Your
Locker

School = lockers!
Finally, a place to express your sense of style *and* organize all your schoolbooks and belongings. We know that school can be super stressful (the tests! the friend groups!), but it's also super fun (the dances! the sports! the LOCKERS!).

RAINBOW LOCKERS?
UMMM CAN WE GO
BACK TO SCHOOL?

easy ways to showcase your style in your locker

HIT THE WALL(PAPER)

Whether it's remnants from your house or your own design on poster board, outline the walls of your locker with a print that pops.

PICTURE THIS

From friends to pets, add photos of the people and places you love so you get an instant boost when you open your locker.

MAKE IT YOURS

Love plants? Add a faux orchid! Have a penchant for purple? Cover the inside with it from head to toe! It's your locker.

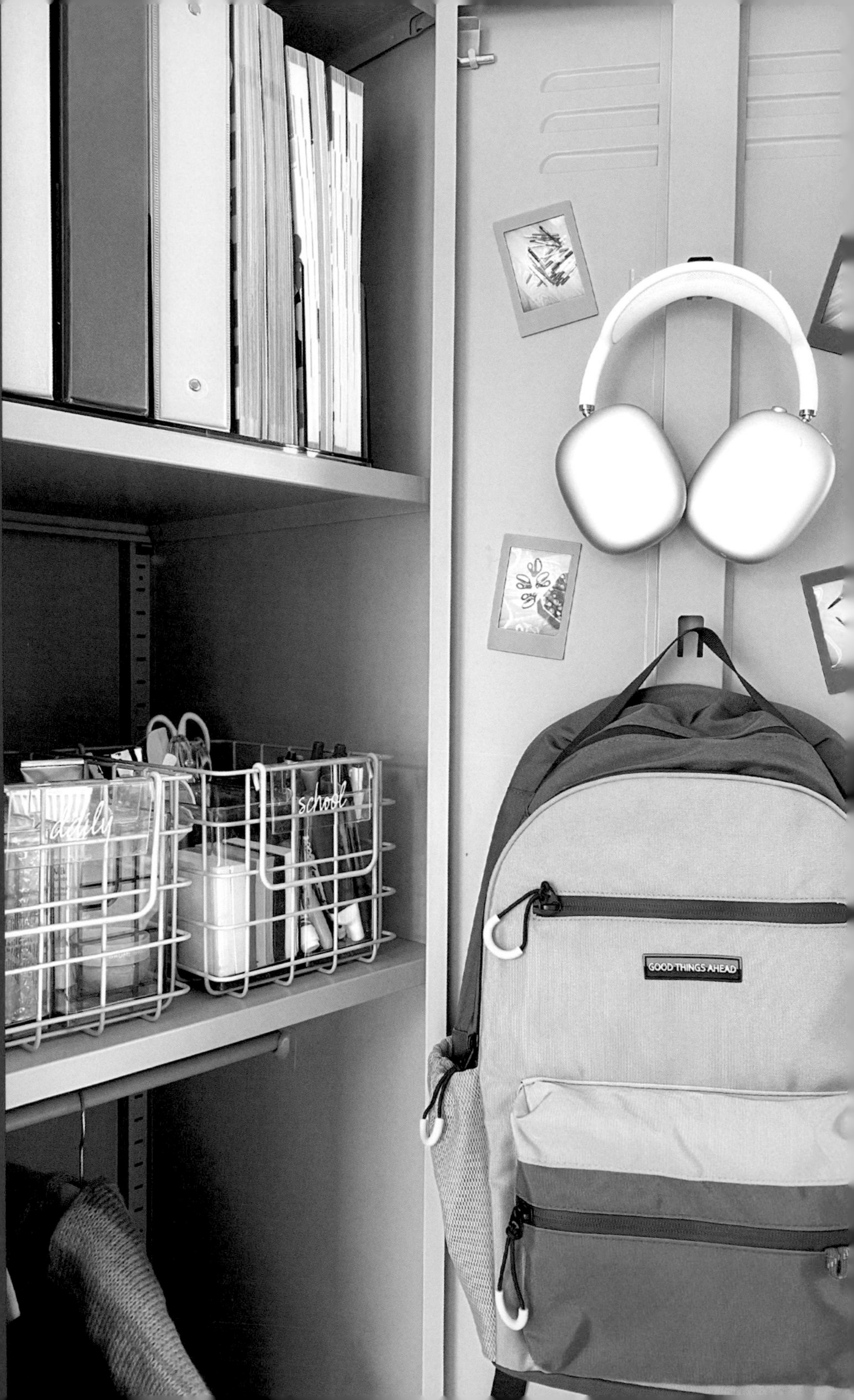
daily
school
GOOD THINGS AHEAD

How To Organize Your Locker

CLEAN SLATE

Like when organizing most spaces, you need to take everything (yes, everything!) out. Those old flyers from the club fair? Recycle them. Pens that don't work? Write this way to the trash can.

DOOR PRIZE

Be sure to utilize the back of your locker door with damage-free hooks for hanging small bags, a lunch box, or headphones, plus lots of magnets for snaps of friends and schedules. (Never forget a test again!)

I SPY

Our number one locker organizing rule: If you can't see it, you can't find it! Organize binders and textbooks with the spines facing outward so you can quickly grab the one you need and go. Be sure to arrange them in the order of your classes to really streamline your day.

CATCH-ALL

Can't find that friendship bracelet? Where is that purple highlighter? Think you put your lip gloss in there? You'll never stress over the little things again with small wire baskets (or even a recycled shoebox!) for those tiny essentials.

HANGING UP

A super-affordable suspension rod will keep sweatshirts and jackets at the ready for those chilly classrooms. Limited on space? Folding works just as well!

BASKET CASE!

Don't lose your marbles (literally!). Containers in your locker, like wire baskets or bins, keep supplies and accessories organized—plus they look supercute.

What's In My Backpack

Here, we unpack the best ways to organize everything you may need in your bag so it's easy to find and easy to maintain, and looks pretty darn cool.

5 WAYS TO PACK A PUNCH IN YOUR BACKPACK

1 First Things First: Edit
You know the drill: Take everything out, down to the granola crumbs and bottle caps at the bottom of your bag.

2 Wash It Out
If you're rocking a well-loved backpack, this is a great time to give it a spin in the washing machine. First read the care instructions or ask someone who knows! Trust us: It will look and feel like a brand-new bag.

3 Think in Color
If you haven't noticed, we're big fans of organizing by color. Not only does it look amazing, but it makes it easier for our minds to process where things are, so you can save those brain cells for your math test!

4 Enlist All the Pouches
We know, we know: You *love* pouches. Same! Organize all the smaller items in your backpack into categories and then assign each one a color, like the purple pouch for skin care (hello, Aquaphor!) and the orange one for writing utensils.

5 Make It Custom

Create a system that works for *you*. For example, it might be easier to organize by day rather than by classes. Or if you're always reaching for your lip gloss, you might want to keep it in the pencil pouch. Create *your* systems for *your* school year!

Desk to Impress

Creating an A+ homework station is easier than social studies! Here, we break down some tips and tricks for a decked-out desk. Don't have everything on the list? No problem! As long as you have a designated spot to tackle your tasks, you are crushing it.

CHOOSE A WORKSPACE

Whether it's a designated room or a rolling cart, having a zone for tackling your homework and to-do list is great for creating a good routine and—rumor has it— some pretty good grades!

CREATE A DROP ZONE

Since not everything needs to go to school every day, assign an area where you can keep your school things organized and easy to grab in a pinch, whether it's a pretty office shelf or a basket in your bedroom.

EXPRESS YOURSELF

Bulletin boards are the easiest ways to tack up photos of friends, inspirational pictures, motivational quotes, and more keepsakes that showcase your POV!

HAVE A SEAT

A sturdy chair makes studying that much more tolerable. We love them on wheels so it's easy to glide and grab papers that are out of reach, but any dining chair will do!

THINK INSIDE THE BOX

From journals to yearbooks, store older documents in a labeled box so they don't get mixed up with current assignments.

DECK OUT YOUR DRAWER

Group everything by category, including notepads, erasers, and writing tools. We *love* to organize pens and markers by color so they are easy to find and easy on the eyes. Don't have a drawer? Put them in a pretty cup instead!

Make a Plan

Nothing feels better on Sunday evening than having a solid game plan for the week. (No unexpected tests or forgotten cleats!) You can write one out in your journal or on a whiteboard. Here's an example:

SCHOOL WEEK AT A GLANCE	TESTS	TASK	ACTIVITIES
MONDAY		BRING BOOK FAIR MONEY	
TUESDAY			SOCCER PRACTICE @4:30
WEDNESDAY	MATH TEST		
THURSDAY		FIELD TRIP FORM DUE	
FRIDAY			SPIRIT DAY!
WEEKEND READY!			
SATURDAY			SLEEPOVER AT ADDISON'S
SUNDAY			LUNCH AT GRANDMA'S

WHAT I'M LOOKING FORWARD TO THIS WEEK

- [ ] BOOK FAIR
- [ ] PEP RALLY ON FRIDAY!
- [ ]
- [ ]

SHOPPING LIST

- [ ] GREEN TOP FOR SPIRIT DAY
- [ ] MORE BLUE PENS
- [ ]
- [ ]

GOLD STAR OF THE WEEK ☆

- [ ] I ORGANIZED MY BATHROOM DRAWER!
- [ ]
- [ ]

Color Correct

Is your phone's home screen a mess? Fear not! We recommend organizing it by color rather than category. Why? Because app icons are intentionally *designed* to be recognized by the brain in a snap. Yet another reason why we love organizing by the rainbow!

 1 **Declutter your screen** and say goodbye to those unused apps.

 2 **Group apps into folders by color.** Tip: Subdivide if you have more of a certain color, like dark orange and light orange.

 3 **Put your most frequently used apps at the very top** so you can spot them immediately. App arrangement within the color folder is a critical part of why this system works!

 4 **The fun part! Pick an emoji that color coordinates** with the apps in the folder, like stars for yellow.

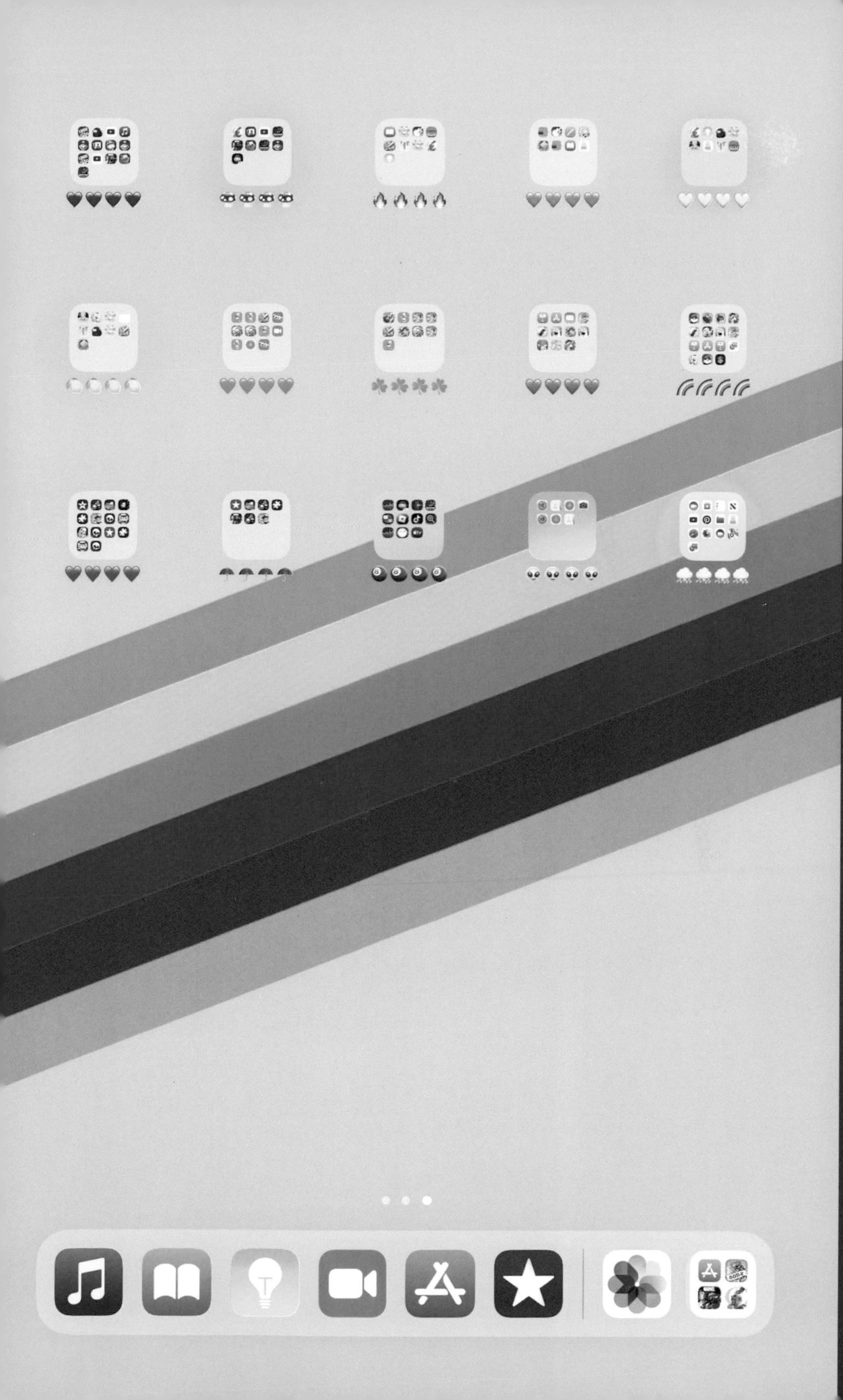

Why Organize by the Rainbow?

Our signature look as organizers has always been color, specifically our affinity for organizing by ROYGBIV (that's

red, orange, yellow, green, blue, indigo, and violet, if you need a refresher on the rainbow!). This is partially a design decision—things in rainbow order look amazing!—but it's also an organizational tool. Our brains innately recognize this pattern, making it faster to find what we're looking for and easier to know where things should be put. Think of it as an organizing cheat sheet!

Let's Do Lunch

Upgrade your meals and your storage so you're never hungry or cleaning unintentional moldy food science experiments again.

SEE YOU LATER, PLASTIC BAGGIES!

Never have a squished sandwich again with a reusable bento box or a piece of Tupperware. (Plus, it's better for the environment!)

EAT YOUR COLORS!

From red cherry tomatoes to beautiful blueberries, these colorful lunch additions are also great brain food!

Snack, Attack!

Get creative (and plan ahead!) with your before- and after-school bites, whether it's a quick grab-and-go breakfast or fuel for volleyball practice.

1 Cookie Time
After a tricky day of multiplication tables (y'all still do those, right?), treat yourself and your sweet tooth by decorating some cookies.

2 S'more the Merrier
Not just for campsites! Nibble on marshmallows, graham crackers, and yummy chocolate after you ace that science quiz.

3 Breakfast of Champions
Is it always a race to get out the door in the morning? Make an oatmeal box the night before so you won't miss this important meal and can eat it in the car or bus.

4 Movie Night
Inspired by our favorite theater snacks, these premade boxes are perfect for backyard movie nights (see page 136).

organizing tasks to tackle!

☆
☆
☆
☆
☆
☆
☆
☆
☆
☆
☆
☆
☆

school goals!

☆

☆

☆

☆

☆

☆

☆

☆

☆

☆

☆

☆

☆

Where You
PLAY

Organizing isn't just about looking "put together" and making your parents happy. (Sidebar: It doesn't make us *unhappy*, but that's beside the point!) Organizing actually makes life *more fun.* Stay with us! Have you ever had to hunt for your tablet tripod to make a video (*It was here last week!*), been unable to find that *pivotal* LEGO piece to complete your masterpiece (*Now it's ruined. Cool, cool.*), or discovered that all your paint pens are dried up just when you need them for an assignment (*Is this where "no cap" started?*)? We can all agree that *this is not fun.* So let's master the mayhem so you can focus on unlocking your creativity and having a good time. We're talking smart storage solutions that make it easy to find your games or art supplies, cool projects to tackle with friends (lemonade stand, anyone?), and more ways to keep clutter at bay and fun at the forefront.

Fun and Games

Game rooms are full of rizz, are we right? (Again, sorry for the rizz comment.) The movie nights! The foosball tournaments! No coasters required! But it's also really, really hard to keep law and order in this super-fun space frequented by buddies. You blink and the next thing you know, the floor is completely covered with loose LEGO bricks, random papers and markers, and spilled popcorn (#cringe). Here's our playbook to help corral the chaos!

organizing playbook!

 If something has been missing a piece for years, we have some bad news: You are not finding that missing piece. Time to toss the rest!

 Haven't played with something in a while but still not ready to part ways? We get it! Put it in a "purge purgatory" box in the garage or basement. If you don't miss it in a few months, then donate it.

 Let's talk about trinkets. Yes, we love them. Yes, they are so (so!) cute when we get them in a party bag. But remember to be an editor when it comes to the small stuff: Do you need eighteen Pop It key chains? Probably not. So pick and organize your faves, then donate the rest.

SCORE SOME BASKETS!

Woven baskets give everything from board games with a million pieces to craft supplies with, also, a million pieces a home so you can spend more time playing and less time searching.

CRAFT CART

To keep the peace with your parents, we suggest putting all the key ingredients for your creative projects on a cart that you can roll in and out when inspiration strikes.

Let's Get Crafty

Never met an art project you didn't like?
It's us, hi! Truly, this is one of the most fun categories to organize by color, whether in an art room, a closet, or even just a cart. The important thing is for everything to have a home so the craft zone feels creative rather than chaotic!

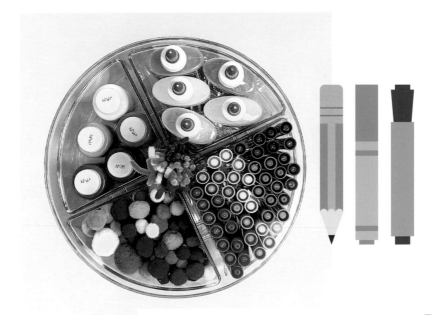

RAINBOW BRIGHT!

Organize pens, markers, and paints by color so they are easy to find (your brain's muscle memory can identify colors in a sec!) and easy to maintain (no more hunting for your favorite colored pen!).

STATE OF THE ART

Put the supplies you don't use every day, like paints and brushes or specific tools, in baskets or boxes and store them until you are ready to make your next masterpiece.

host a lemonade stand!

Calling all entrepreneurs! Create a successful lemonade stand with your pals and learn about sales, marketing, and the joys of earning money as well as donating to a good cause. As always, being organized with your setup (line up those cups!) and your business plan (people are most likely to stop on Sundays!) will make the experience more successful *and* more fun!

shopping list

☐ Lemonade mix

☐ Fresh lemons

☐ Water

☐ Pitcher

☐ Cups

☐ Décor (sign, balloons, etc.)

☐ Folding table or homemade stand

☐ Tablecloth (optional)

☐ Cashbox and change

☐ Sweet treats

☐ Ice

SWEETEN THE DEAL WITH FRESH CUPCAKES!

ICEBREAKER

Don't forget to have extra ice on hand (we promise, you're going to need it!).

MAKING BANK

Be sure to have change ready to break big bills!

LET'S ORGANIZE . . .

MARKETING PLAN

So you have a great product (the best lemonade in town!), and now you need to sell it. Here are some simple (and fun!) tips for success:

- [ ] Make colorful signs to advertise the sale and post them at nearby street intersections (be careful if they're busy!). Be sure to include the date, time, and price.

- [ ] Create handheld signs for the location of sale.

- [ ] Be heard! Be sure to be friendly and shout your offerings.

- [ ] Increase your visibility with balloons and streamers!

- [ ] Is there a cause that some or all of the proceeds support? Let the customers know!

Create a
Content Corner

Do you love creating and sharing makeup videos? Do you choreograph dance routines with your friends? Carve out some space to let your creativity shine! And though it goes without saying (but as moms, we're going to say it again!), *always* talk to your parents first about what you choose to share on the internet.

BRIGHT IDEA! SET UP A RING LIGHT IN THE CORNER TO UPGRADE YOUR VIDEOS.

WONDERWALL

Get as many things as possible off the floor! This way, tennis rackets or soccer balls are easy to find, there are no tripping hazards (been there), and you save *so much time* before practice.

Play Ball!

School is the season of sports. And we're talking *all the sports*. Basketball, volleyball, lacrosse (why is the equipment so bulky?!), cheerleading, football, and, and, and. We could go on! Just so you know, we don't know a ton about #sports except that our kids play them, and corralling the cleats is a whole thing (especially when you're already late for school!). Okay, mom rant over. Let's make mornings easier for everyone with clear systems for whatever sports era you're in!

HAVE A BALL

Basketballs, baseballs, tennis balls, Wiffle balls, you name it! There are so many balls for all the #sports you play, so keep them in a basket so spotting what you need is a cinch.

DON'T FORGET!

Have an air pump at the ready so your pickup basketball game plans aren't deflated.

organizing tasks to tackle!

☆

☆

☆

☆

☆

☆

☆

☆

☆

☆

☆

☆

☆

activity goals!

☆

☆

☆

☆

☆

☆

☆

☆

☆

☆

☆

☆

☆

Where You DREAM

Unlike the living room (*How many throw pillows does a sofa need?*) or dining room (*Uncomfortable dining chairs? Neat.*), your bedroom is your special space! It's the one room in the house where you can express your distinct point of view, whether through the color of the walls or the photos on your bulletin board. So let your self-expression—not piles of clothes or scattered art projects—take center stage in your sanctuary with some super-simple systems that will keep you organized while spotlighting your style.

Dress Up Your Closet

Closets can be a bigger headache than homework. *Where's my statement headband? Has anyone seen my favorite top? Do I have to hang up my clothes AGAIN?* We hear you. We see you. And we have a plan! Follow our checklist to transform your chaotic closet (and while we're here, those dramatic drawers!) into a boutique-inspired space.

closet checklist

Use this cheat sheet to conquer your closet. You got this!

☐ **TAKE IT OUT**

Remove every. single. item. from your closet. Yes, even those random spirit sticks from the pep rally. Yes, even that mystery storage bin on the top shelf that's been there since you were in kindergarten.

☐ **EDIT**

Do you really need that school T-shirt from four years ago? Make a donation pile for everything you've outgrown, including clothes, shoes, socks, underwear, and pajamas.

☐ **ASSIGN CATEGORIES**

Wow—you got rid of so much! Next, sort everything into categories, like clothes to hang, clothes to fold, seasonal items (swimsuits, #sports stuff, etc.), purses, backpacks, headbands, and shoes.

☐ **STICK WITH A SYSTEM**

Do you like to hang everything, or do you find folding clothes easier? Do you like your footwear on a shelf or in a shoe organizer hanging on a door? Pick a system that makes maintaining your closet a breeze. For example, if hanging up pants isn't your jam, now is a great time to pivot to folded stacks.

☐ **PUT IT ON DISPLAY**

For accessories, like clutches, hats, and headbands, display them (like at a store!) so you always know where they are *and* you have a stylish shelf. Who says closets can't be cute?

 Date Completed: _____

Closet Confidential

From hangers to shelves, there are countless ways to make your closet a space where you feel like you're shopping for a cute outfit every morning (even if you wear uniforms!). Here, we dish our organizing secrets.

Hang in there with super-slim felt hangers that fit double the amount of clothes in your closet.

Save hanging space (and time!) and fold sweaters and sweatshirts.

Showcase—and keep track of—your cool sneaker collection. (Limited shelf space? Opt for an over-the-door shoe organizer instead.)

Create a display of your favorite bags, headbands, and bobbles that look pretty clutch.

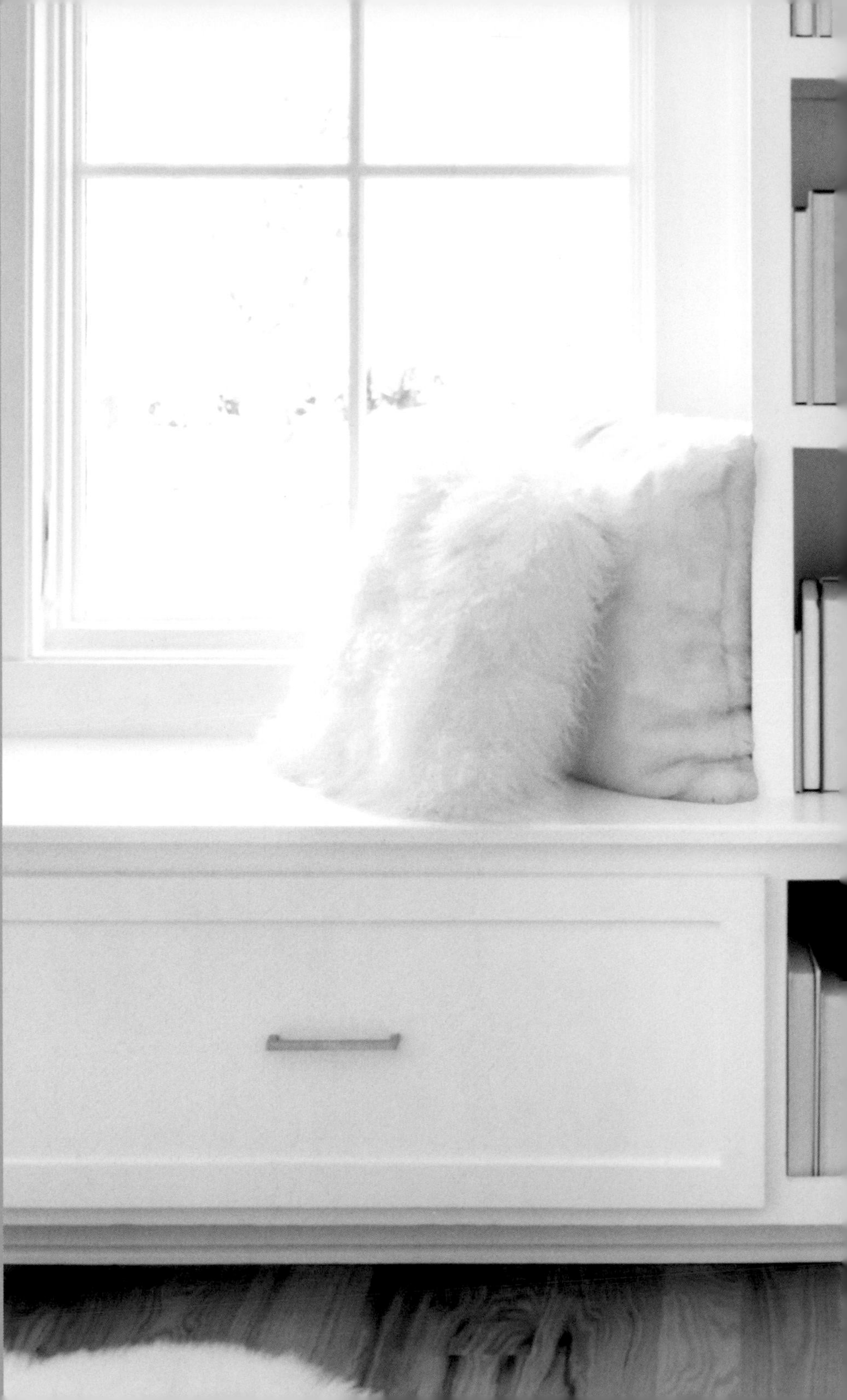

Did you know that dollhouses provide plenty of storage opportunities? Who knew! This one is in Stella's bedroom, where she uses it to stash extra blankets and a basket of dolls. (It's the "vintage" phone for us.)

Deck the Door!

Whether you share a closet with a sibling or you're just limited on storage options in your bedroom, take advantage of the most underappreciated zone in the room: the back of your door! Seriously, it's a super hard worker (with the right caddy, it can store *so much!*).

SHOES ALWAYS GET LOST IN THE SHUFFLE, SO KEEP THEM IN SIGHT BEHIND YOUR DOOR.

Just
for Kicks!

Shoes are just the best, no matter how old you are! And especially if your school has uniforms or a strict dress code, sometimes it's the only way to showcase your unique style. Whether your closet has shoe rails, empty shelves you aren't using, or an over-the-door shoe organizer, put your best foot forward by organizing (and spotlighting) your favorite pairs.

A SHOE-IN!

You know we love to ROYGBIV anything we touch, and shoes are no exception! We recommend organizing by color within each category, like sneakers, dress shoes, sandals, and slippers.

ACCESSORY ZONE!

We see you, Swifties! Y'all *love* your friendship bracelets, and accessories in general. We do too! Keep them organized in a designated drawer so they don't disappear in the wash or vanish behind a dresser.

BOY MEETS WORLD

From ties to suspenders, store special-occasion pieces that you don't use every day in a specific drawer or basket so you won't lose them (or annoy your 'rents when you frantically hunt for them two minutes before you need to leave!).

REPEAT AFTER US: DRESSERS ARE YOUR FRIEND! BELTS TEND TO GET TANGLED IN CLOSETS (OR DISAPPEAR), SO WRAP THEM UP AND STORE THEM IN A DRAWER.

Store the "Stuff"

Let the record show: *We aren't anti-stuff!* You have a lot of things that are important to you, so they are important to us. Friendship bracelets, to-be-used stickers, video game accessories for game nights with your friends, and on and on and on. So give all your special belongings in your bedroom a proper home, like a designated drawer or basket, so you can easily find them and they don't appear to be just a pile of stuff (they aren't!).

GAME ON!

If you're a gamer, create a space to keep all the accessories, controls, and gizmos so you're not holding up the game looking for those missing headphones.

That's Your Jam

Go put your records on! With screens and streaming literally everywhere now, carve out a little corner where you can enjoy some of your favorite tunes. (And if a song strikes a chord, grab your guitar and play along!) Not musically inclined? Easily pivot to create a cozy reading nook!

balancing act

We all love creating and watching content, but it's also important to make time to shut off our screens. (Sorry, don't be mad at us!)

USE SCREEN TIME LIMITS

If you're spending more time on your phone than with friends and family, it's time to put it down.

SCHEDULE SCREEN-FREE ACTIVITIES

Leave your devices at home (or at least in your bag!) and have fun watching a movie or playing a game.

TAKE IT OUTSIDE

Like, right now. Go! Whether it is doing a cannonball into a swimming pool or jumping on a trampoline, get some vitamin D.

Calm, Cool, and Collected

From LEGO masterpieces to limited-edition basketball cards (that are "investments, Mom!"), your special projects and collectibles merit a spot to shine or MVP storage so you can cherish them for years (and years!).

HOUSE OF CARDS

Keep your trading cards in mint condition (no wrinkles or creases here!) in binders that you can organize by team, players, or value. Yay, #sports!

LOVE IT TO PIECES

Pick your most prized projects, like this *impressive* Death Star (Is that what this is? Whatever, you get it!) on a shelf to be admired. Plus, it doubles as décor!

TIP: Do your parents, siblings, and—most important—yourself a favor: Store extra LEGO pieces you aren't using in a bin or ziplock bag so there aren't any tears when someone steps on a rogue piece.

seasonal

LET'S ORGANIZE . . .

In-N-Out Storage

We all have items that are heavy hitters for a season: Swimsuits and cover-ups are the leading actors in the summer months, then take a bow and exit stage left by September. **(Sweaters, enter stage right.)** Designate a large basket (or baskets if you have the space) to keep on the top shelf of your closet or under your bed to rotate these seasonal staples so they aren't taking up valuable space when they clock out.

MAXIMIZE STORAGE IN OUT-OF-SIGHT AREAS, LIKE UNDER THE BED, FOR ITEMS THAT YOU DON'T UTILIZE EVERY DAY.

organizing tasks to tackle!

☆

☆

☆

☆

☆

☆

☆

☆

☆

☆

☆

☆

☆

bedroom goals!

☆
☆
☆
☆
☆
☆
☆
☆
☆
☆
☆
☆
☆
☆

Where You

The bathroom is where you start and end your day, so let's make it a place that's both functional (everything is easy to find!) and also fun (organized by color!). And we get it—even in our own bathrooms, the struggle is *real* when it comes to wrangling makeup, skin care, hair products— essentially everything and the bathroom sink! Trust us: Following these easy steps will bring order to your countertops and a smile to your face every time you open your drawers.

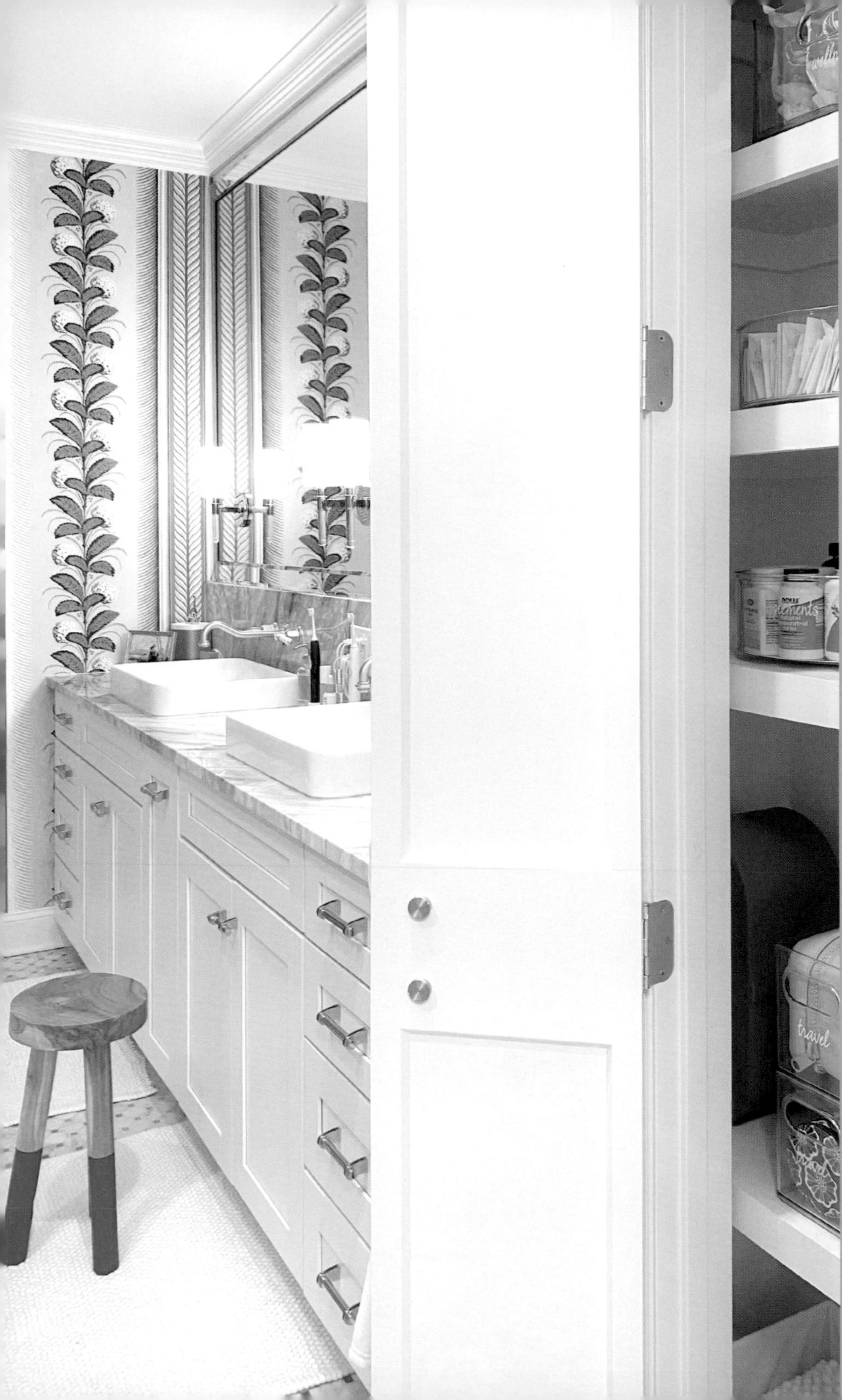
travel

GET YOUR
HEAD IN THE GAME

We (aka Joanna) are obsessed with headbands. They truly are the easiest way to dress up an outfit or combat a bad hair day. Running late? Throw on a headband! We love putting them on display so it's easy to grab one and go.

Hair-Raising Org!

The amount of stuff that comes with washing, styling, and accessorizing hair would give anyone a headache. The products! The potions! The headbands! The list goes on and on (and on and on). But while it might seem like the biggest chore to organize and maintain all that stuff, it's actually a lot of fun. *This is not a trap!* Seriously, by transforming your bathroom drawers and countertops, you can make the most mundane morning feel like an appointment at the beauty bar. (Cucumber water is encouraged but not necessary!)

A SEPARATE PEACE

Identify your go-to hair categories, like accessories, then create groupings within each category, like scrunchies and hair clips. The simple secret here is to separate the items in the groups. No hair ties should ever mingle with the round brush!

Let It Sink In

1

For toilet paper, Q-Tips, and other paper and cotton products

2

For extra body wash, shampoo, conditioner, and sunscreen

The cabinet underneath the sink can fill you with dread: *What's even under there? Aren't there, like, pipes and stuff?* This underutilized space can easily become a black hole for products, towels, and random accessories never to be seen again. Until now! **Here, we show you four ways to transform this space.**

3

For bath linens, like towels and washcloths

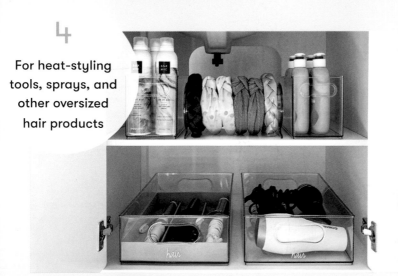

4

For heat-styling tools, sprays, and other oversized hair products

Daily Drawer

If you do only one organizing project in the bathroom, *this is the one to do.* The daily drawer is your bathroom bestie, featuring the greatest hits of your routine that you use twice a day. We're talking about your toothpaste, hairbrush, facial cleansing wipes—the things you reach for the most. Having them in a designated spot makes them easy to grab, easy to put away, and easy to keep off your countertops.

SPACE JAMS

Arrange your heavy hitters in the drawer to keep wet items, like toothbrushes and toothpaste, away from dry items, like cotton swabs.

PRO TIP

Do you share a bathroom and don't get a drawer? A daily bin that fits neatly on the countertop or under the sink works just as well!!

GREAT WALL!

If you're limited on drawer space (or share a bathroom with siblings—#ugh), hit your walls with simple floating shelves to store your most-loved products. (Organized by color, obvi.)

Prep School: A.M. Routine

You don't want to be running around trying to find your go-to sunscreen (*No not that one, the other one!*) or track down your favorite moisturizer (*It was here yesterday, wasn't it?*) before school. Create a daily checklist to streamline your morning.

☐ **1 Wash Your Face!**
Whether it's in the shower or using micellar water on a cotton pad, start your day with a clean canvas. Remember to keep your face wash in the same designated spot in a drawer or in the shower. Cluttered countertops? Not here!

☐ **2 Sink Your Teeth Into It**
Know what's not cool? Bad breath and cavities. Assign a spot for your toothbrush, floss, and mouthwash so these frequent fliers are within easy reach.

☐ **3 Hair Care**
Organize the OGs, like your brush, sprays, and ties, in your daily drawer or bin so you can save time in the morning by not having to rummage through a trove of products you don't use on the reg.

☐ **4 Makeup**
Simplify your school makeup routine, if you have one, by keeping the essentials in a designated drawer or pouch. Reminder: This is a super-fun step, but by no means a necessary one. Y'all are beautiful!

Prep School: P.M. Routine

What. a. day. From working hard in class to leaving it all on the practice field, school can be *exhausting*. Which means it's easy to cut corners at night: *I'll wash my face in the morning. I can't even find a clean towel.* Our tip: Create a ridiculously simple nighttime routine that you actually look forward to. Here's how. 👍

turn your nighttime routine into a vibe*

 Turn on an essential oil diffuser to create a super-chill experience. Don't have one? Do a spritz of a refreshing room spray to create a serene scene.

 Play your favorite music on low while you wash your face, brush your teeth, etc. Plus, research shows that listening to music can reduce stress. Score!

 Finish with a sixty-second edit. Quickly clear the countertops and tuck in all your products for the night. Morning you will love nighttime you!

*Did we use "vibe" right?

In the Fold

Learning to fold a towel is like learning to ride a bike or drive a car: It's a rite of passage and an invaluable skill. Here, we break it down step-by-step. Warning: Favorite child status is headed your way!

1 **It's time to throw in the towel!** Gather all your towels (and donate any that have seen better days).

2 **Lay out a towel on the floor or a bed.**

PRO TIP: Store towels in baskets so there are no falling towers!

3 Fold the right side of the towel toward the center.

4 Next, fold the left side of the towel over the right side.

5 From the top, fold down to the center of the towel.

6 Repeat step 5 to the bottom of the towel. You did it! You now have a neat and compact towel that is ready for any adventure.

Caddy
Shack

Is there anything worse when you are taking a shower than to realize your favorite face wash is not in the shower but on the countertop *one million miles away?* We'll wait. That dreaded feeling will be a distant memory with a stocked and organized shower caddy.

Yes, we are all guilty of putting our products on the shower floor or around the tub. And yes, we have all accidentally knocked them over and stubbed our toes. Until now! Bring those products up so you never again have to look down and scream, "Ouch!"

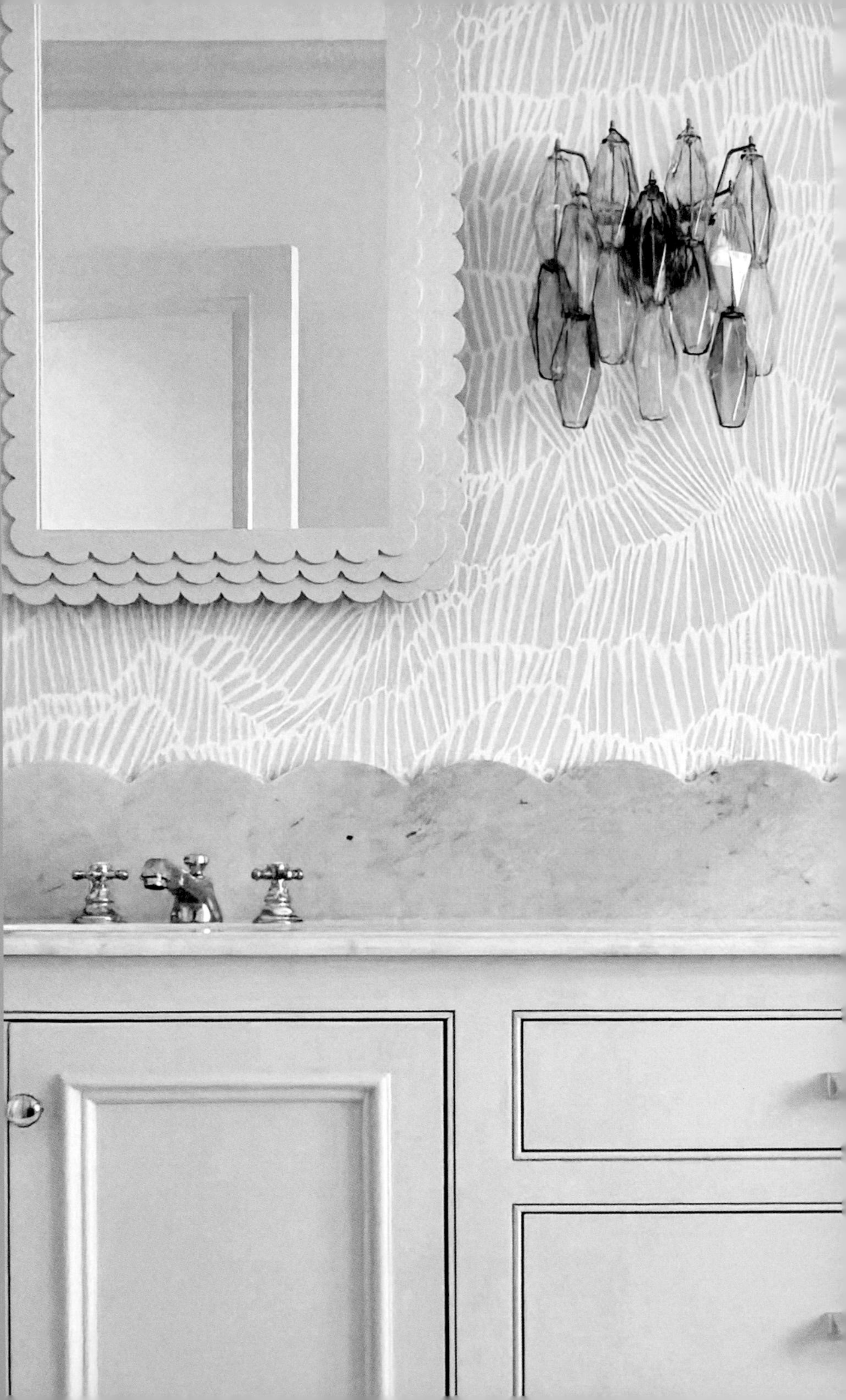

DOUBLE DUTY

We get it: Sharing a space, *especially a bathroom*, can sometimes not be ideal. Pro tip: Get special towels, whether monogrammed or a designated color, so you never confuse them for your siblings'.

organizing tasks to tackle!

☆

☆

☆

☆

☆

☆

☆

☆

☆

☆

☆

☆

☆

daily goals!

☆

☆

☆

☆

☆

☆

☆

☆

☆

☆

☆

☆

☆

Where You  *CELEBRATE*

Get your playlist ready: From sleepovers to pool parties, we're breaking down how to host a fun get-together with all of the streamers and none of the stress. We've said it before, and we're saying it again: Organizing isn't just about things looking a certain way (though that's a bonus). It's about creating streamlined systems, like snack zones for your slumber party or movie night, so you can spend less time worrying about the details and more time celebrating with your besties.

host an epic sleepover!

MAKE IT PERSONAL

Give each space a special touch with your bestie's name and some of their favorite things that double as party favors.

Your friends are coming! Your friends are coming! Whether it's for your big birthday bash or another special occasion (Galentine's Day!), outfit your sleepover space with everything you and your guests need for an awesome night that is anything but a snooze.

party prep list

MAKE THE GUEST LIST

Be sure to be inclusive and not leave anyone out! Also, ask your friends if they have any allergies or medical conditions, and tell your parents. Like, Kennedy can't eat peanuts or Blake sometimes needs an inhaler.

CREATE AN INVITATION

This can be handmade and delivered in person or as a texted digital flyer. Get creative! If there is a theme, like "Pack Your Trunk for Camp Collins!" then showcase it here.

STOCK UP

Make a shopping list of everything you'll need. Snacks? (There can never be too many!) Are y'all making a craft? Get all your supplies a couple of days before the event so you have time to get them organized and ready to go. (No one wants to deal with bulky packaging at the party!)

DRAFT AN AGENDA

This is the fun part! Ideas include crafting friendship bracelets, having a make-your-own pizza dinner, watching a movie, and—for whoever is still awake— telling scary stories with a flashlight! (Actually, can we come?) But remember: Don't be too rigid with the schedule. If an epic hide-and-seek game is running long, enjoy the moment and ignore the clock!

PLAN YOUR SPACE

If there are a lot of attendees and sleeping bags are required, you may want to rework the furniture arrangement in your bedroom or living room. That way, you won't be panicking when there isn't a place for Sally to sleep.

Lights, Camera, Movie Night!

There's nothing like watching a movie with friends and family *outside*! It just makes the experience so much more magical, right? And it's *so easy*. You can go all out with a popcorn machine, or keep it simple with a self-serve snack station. Plus, the price of projectors starts at fifty dollars (the price of roughly four movie tickets!). So if you don't have one, this is a great addition to your birthday or holiday wish list.

set the scene

CONCESSIONS

A mix of salty and sweet snacks is always a hit.

STAR-STUDDED DÉCOR

From marquee-style letter lights to handmade movie posters announcing the feature film, these easy layers add some serious movie magic to the night.

BEST SEATS IN THE HOUSE

Rearrange outdoor furniture to face the projection, or simply lay down a ton of blankets and pillows to create a super-cozy pallet that's perfect for movie watching *and* stargazing.

top 5 movie recs

These fun flicks are sure to be crowd-pleasers!

THE PARENT TRAP

Bonus points if you learn the secret handshake between Annie and Martin.

MATILDA

We can't choose a favorite between the '90s movie version and the 2022 musical. DON'T MAKE US.

THE LEGO MOVIE

Get ready for "Everything is awesome!" to be stuck in your head in the best possible way.

HARRY POTTER AND THE SORCERER'S STONE

Wands, a sorting hat, and butterbeers are encouraged for this magical viewing.

HOME ALONE

Clea's family is so obsessed with this movie, we watch it even when it's *not* the holidays.

host a pool party!

Provide some colorful towels for your friends (that double as a reusable party favor!).

Pool Parties that Make a *Splash!*

Is there anything more fun than swimming with your besties on a superhot summer day? (We agree, there's not!) Whether it's at your house or your local community pool, have some fun in the sun with an easy-breezy pool party, complete with games and lots of sunscreen.

A CART IS PERFECT FOR AN AT-HOME PARTY SO ALL YOUR SUPPLIES ARE EASY TO WHEEL IN TO GRAB, THEN WHEEL OUT TO STORE.

Don't forget to apply (and reapply!) your sunscreen every two hours. There's no easier way to ruin a party than with a sunburn!

Party Time (Anytime!)

No more scattered supplies around the house! Have everything for your next party organized in designated drawers so you can instantly be the ultimate host without hunting for the party blowers.

BIN THERE

Drawers + bins = best friends forever. Small containers keep your categories separate so you can find what you need. Plus, it's easy to find makeshift bins around the house. (An iPhone box can do wonders!)

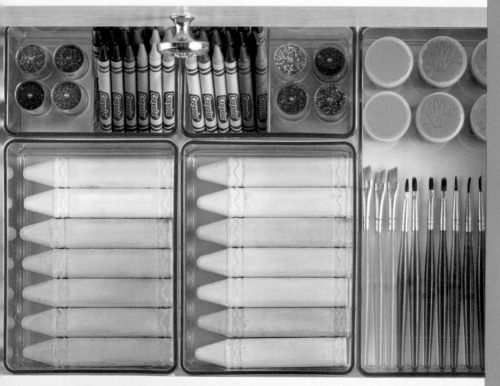

organizing tasks to tackle!

☆
☆
☆
☆
☆
☆
☆
☆
☆
☆
☆
☆
☆
☆

party goals!

☆

☆

☆

☆

☆

☆

☆

☆

☆

☆

☆

☆

☆

Where You
GO

Did someone say road trip? Va-ca-tion, all we ever wanted! And know what we love almost as much as taking a trip? *Planning outfits* and *packing* for a trip! Whether you're getting ready to go to camp for a couple of weeks (reminder: you only get *one trunk*) or wheels up with your fam for a summer vacay (window seat, please), these space- and sanity-saving tips will ensure that you make memories on your adventures, rather than fretting over your forgotten swimsuit bottoms or favorite pair of shoes.

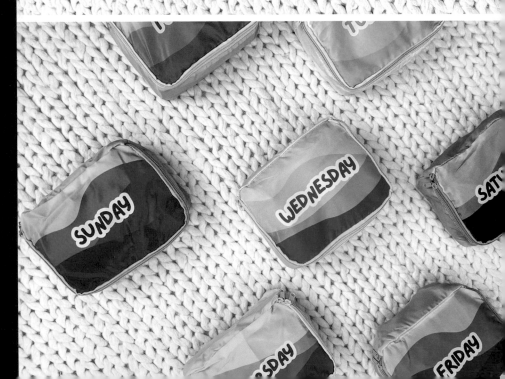

Leader of the Pack!

Humble brag alert: We are expert packers (and we see your bombastic* side-eye!). But hey—you're going to be an expert too with these super-easy tips that make packing an absolute delight. (The outfit planning is the best!) Here are the tried-and-true steps to a perfectly packed suitcase that keeps everything contained even when you're on the go.

STEP 1

Packing cubes are a game changer for your suitcase, duffel, or trunk. Plus, they make packing *and* unpacking so much easier. Don't have packing cubes? NBD! Gallon ziplock bags work just as well and are easy to label.

STEP 2

After folding your clothes, stand them on end upright rather than stacking them so you can clearly see what you have (and don't have to take *everything* out on day one because you couldn't find your favorite top).

STEP 3

Organizing packing cubes by the days of the week is a great idea, *especially* if you are going on a longer trip with multiple destinations (Grandma's for two nights before the beach!). We've all been there where the suitcase looks like an explosion by day three.

STEP 4

Designate a larger packing cube (or an extra duffel bag you can fold at the bottom of your suitcase) for worn clothes so you don't have to air dirty laundry throughout your trip.

*Okay, what does this actually mean?

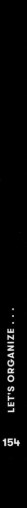

TRUNK SHOW

Trunks aren't just for summer adventures! They double as storage at the foot of your bed when camp isn't in session.

Let's Go to Camp!

The highlight of summer for a lot of you is sleepaway camp. The friendships! The s'mores! No parents! (*We know y'all miss us, right?*) But packing for camp is a big deal. There are no trips to the store once you get there because you forgot your water shoes. We break down what to pack (and how to pack!) for camp in the next few pages.

camp packing list

Start with your camp's suggested packing list and go from there. We recommend you start packing (or at a minimum, writing out your list) at least two weeks before you leave so you can be prepared and ready to go! Here's a good place to get started:

☐ **OUTFITS**

Check your camp's activities list and how many nights you'll be gone and build your daily outfits from there. Essentials include everyday clothes, swimsuits, cover-ups, tennis shoes, shower flip-flops, pajamas, underwear, and special outfits for—*squeal*—dances!

☐ **TOILETRIES**

Toothpaste, toothbrush, floss, shampoo, conditioner, soap, razors, a hairbrush, bug spray, and sunscreen are the big ones. When it comes to beauty products, pack sparingly. (There's a very good chance that someone in your cabin will also have hairspray.)

☐ **BED LINENS**

Pack a pillow and a sleeping bag, plus two fitted sheets and two pillowcases. Don't forget your favorite stuffed animal or blanket to make your bunk feel like home!

☐ **RAIN GEAR**

Be sure to include a rain jacket and waterproof shoes for those inevitable wet days. Wet bags are also great to have on hand, especially on overnight camping trips.

☐ **FUN SUPPLIES**

Don't forget stationery (paper, pens, stamped envelopes) for writing letters home or a flashlight (with extra batteries!) for telling ghost stories.

Adventure Awaits!

Whether you are a seasoned camper or gearing up for your first year, here are our top packing tips for a summer you'll never forget.

IN THE CLEAR

We recommend clear bins so that (1) you can see all the contents and easily grab what you need without creating chaos and (2) you can slide the bins under your bed or onto your designated camp shelf.

GOT YOUR BACK

Remember, not *every single thing* needs to go inside your trunk (especially if you're flying to camp). Use your backpack to keep your OG essentials on hand, from a water bottle to chargers.

Make the call on travel-size versus full-size products based on the length of your stay. (You don't need a full bottle of shampoo for just a weekend!)

What's Up, Dopp (Kit)?

When packing for a trip, you want to make sure that you properly stock your toiletry bag or dopp kit. (Running out of bug spray on a camping trip sounds like a nightmare!) We suggest finding a waterproof travel bag that has lots of compartments so it's easy to see and easy to store your essentials.

camp letter to home

_____

_____

_____

_____

_____

_____

_____

_____

_____

_____

_____

_____

_____

_____

_____

_____

_____

_____

_____

_____

_____

_____

adventure goals!

☆
☆
☆
☆
☆
☆
☆
☆
☆
☆
☆
☆
☆
☆

organizing report card

Don't worry—this isn't a regular report card. (If you're reading this, you've passed with flying rainbow colors!)

Use this sheet to keep track of your progress throughout the book!

CHAPTER

 **GLOW LIST**
(What I Rocked!)

WHERE YOU LEARN *Star Rating:* ☆☆☆☆☆	
WHERE YOU PLAY *Star Rating:* ☆☆☆☆☆	
WHERE YOU DREAM *Star Rating:* ☆☆☆☆☆	
WHERE YOU PREP *Star Rating:* ☆☆☆☆☆	
WHERE YOU CELEBRATE *Star Rating:* ☆☆☆☆☆	
WHERE YOU GO *Star Rating:* ☆☆☆☆☆	

Name: _____

Age: _____

Date: _____

🍕 GROW LIST
(What I'll Try!)

💶 FAVORITE THINGS I ACCOMPLISHED

THE
notebook

Feeling inspired? Use the next few pages
to doodle and jot down your dreams,
ideas, and goals!

THANKS! ♡

Thank you, as always, to our incredible team at The Home Edit and Hello Sunshine for supporting us every step of the way. To our incredible publishing team at Clarkson Potter—Mia Johnson, Kim Tyner, Abby Oladipo, Brianne Sperber, Natalie Yera-Campbell, Darian Keels, Aaron Wehner—and to Cait Hoyt, our literary agent, and Angelin Adams, our editor, for guiding us so masterfully through our fourth book together! An extra special thank-you to Shaina Burrell, Hillary Franchi, Larry and Wendy Ngyuen, and Jeanne Lyons Davis for their superhuman abilities in making this book come together. From creative and art direction to content and editing, this book would not have happened without your involvement. And thank you to our community for making our dreams a reality. The Home Edit wouldn't be the same without you, and we are so glad you are here.

From Joanna: To my mom for believing that I could become literally anything in my life, including a professional organizer—although my high school bedroom would certainly say otherwise.

From Clea: Thank you to my mom, who would never have let my room get messy in the first place.

index

Published in the United States by Clarkson Potter/Publishers, an imprint of the Crown Publishing Group, a division of Penguin Random House LLC, New York.
Clarkson Potter.com

CLARKSON POTTER is a trademark and POTTER with colophon is a registered trademark of Penguin Random House LLC.

Library of Congress Cataloging-in-Publication Data

Names: Shearer, Clea, 1982–author. | Teplin, Joanna, 1979–author.
Title: The home edit: ready, set, organize! : a guide to editing your space, expressing your style, and getting things done / Clea Shearer and Joanna Teplin.
Description: New York : Clarkson Potter, [2024] | Includes index. | Audience: Grades 4–6
Identifiers: LCCN 2023057721 (print) | LCCN 2023057722 (ebook) | ISBN 9780593712221 (hardcover) | ISBN 9780593712238 (ebook)
Subjects: LCSH: Storage in the home—Juvenile literature. | Orderliness—Juvenile literature.
Classification: LCC TX309 .S48 2024 (print) | LCC TX309 (ebook) | DDC 648/.8—dc23/eng/20240229
LC record available at https://lccn.loc.gov/2023057721
LC ebook record available at https://lccn.loc.gov/2023057722

ISBN 978-0-593-71222-1
Ebook ISBN 978-0-593-71223-8

Printed in China

Editor: Angelin Adams
Editorial assistant: Darian Keels
Designer: Outfit Branding & Design
Design manager: Christina Self
Art director: Mia Johnson
Production editor: Abby Oladipo
Production manager: Kim Tyner
Prepress color manager: Neil Spitkovsky
Compositor: Merri Ann Morrell
Copyeditor: Diana Drew
Proofreader: Andrea Peabbles
Indexer: Elise Hess
Publicist: Natalie Yera-Campbell
Marketer: Brianne Sperber

10 9 8 7 6 5 4 3 2 1

First Edition